DEMOLITION

OF THE

PROMISED

LAND

POEMS BY
ERIN KEANE

Demolition of the Promised Land

poems by
Erin Keane

TYPECAST
PUBLISHING

ISBN 978-0-9844961-7-4

Typecast Publishing
241 Pinners Cove Road
Asheville, NC 28803

Cover design by Larry Buchanan
Text design by Jen Woods

Printed in the United States of America

CONTENTS

CONTENTS

For Drew, always.

A Chemistry Exam Cheat Sheet

It's just liquids and solids and kinetics and
solutions so relax: think construction crews,
wrecking balls, Saturday night in the rearview,
the reaction of fight, love, flight. In five words
or less, predict your chance for escape. Imagine
you and you and you, a tangle of smoke and
knees and *Birth of the Cool*—name the one
in the cat's-eye glasses who spilled a drink down
her maroon silk dress. Will she send the future
you a message by text, and what will it say?
True or false: *Dopamine* is a sick Baltimore DJ,
Xanax a Japanese comic for girls. Explain
Chicago. Define a glass platform five layers
thick, suspended in mid-air, take that one step
into nothing (rate of change, distance with time) then
divide by x, the slick neoprene black hole
of everything that keeps and changes: records
of once-upon-a-time teeth and their lonely
crowns, those spare forensic hairs. What's left?
The burning question, for extra credit: Will you love
me tomorrow? And will I? Craft a plausible
hypothesis, you optimist. Outline an experiment
in which you go to bed then get up every day
until you don't. Your data is all we have,
so be honest. Repeat as needed. Show your work.

PART ONE

A Supermarket in New Jersey

The monks are setting themselves on fire, and the bees
have all but disappeared. Last night
Bruce Springsteen went to the supermarket—

the fancy one near his house, where
mangoes piled high like dragon eggs make him forget
the news. He pushes his red shopping cart
into the mortuary glow of the yogurt case,
the wheels impossibly smooth, this Bentley
of a cart full of snacks, and considers the tubs—
what to do about the honey flavor, he wonders,
about the taste of golden summer

depleted. Abundance is a mirage—
the monks know that. There are no poets
in the fruit. The wives are still in the avocados,
but he knows better than to write about them.
The sushi guy chops tuna belly,
a Chopin sonata. Children at this hour
are mostly pliant: shy grins
when Bruce Springsteen draws bananas like six-shooters,
tries to play O. K. Corral in the aisle, wishing he had
a cowboy hat. Popping like flashbulbs

under soft, overhead light, here are five different kinds
of grape, and for a second he finds himself
thinking, *What could go wrong*
in a world with five different kinds of grape?
Honeybees lost and the crops just go?

To say nothing of the harvest—children in the tomatoes.

Boys drink oil to explode from within
on main streets, in markets.
What would I burn for?
Bruce Springsteen wonders,
when he knows only the comfort
of the six-inch valley, the dull knife's desire.

It is Peep season. Little armies
of chicken-shaped fluff, their sugared,
baleful stares. It is quiet, aside
from refrigerators humming and the tender
mist of water over the greens.

You can't price a kerosene fire by weight,
Bruce Springsteen murmurs,
pats his pocket for a pencil, thinks,
That's a good one, save.

Forgive me, Walt Whitman, I called to you.
There ain't no Eden in this Garden State.

West Kentucky Heartbreak

—for Jason Joyce

For years, I have watched the redbuds unfurl
on this cratered parkway and never once stopped

in Muhlenberg County to say hello to the Everlys,
never lingered in Rosine at Bill Monroe's barn.

My sins against rock & roll confessed, and now this
radio silence, these vinyl school bus seats bereft

of paperclip etchings—your name, the year, oh,
plain artifact: once, you were here, singing along

with Hank when he saw the gasping light and little
planes skidded like needles across old records.

Some things we can't bear to see—how the trees
keep budding without missing a beat. And your name—

traced in the dust on a dry-docked fastback
waiting on an engine, scratched in the roller rink

while "Stairway to Heaven" skates sweethearts
backwards, disco ball dappling their clasped hands,

scrawled on the case of a vintage Gibson sighing
by the stage in the dilatory hours before a show,

your name. On the cover of *#1 Record*, with a photo
of you and me at thirteen in all our terrified glory.

Your name on the Graceland wall, the Killer's bench,
the pews in the hallowed Ryman. Your name, God

help me, along the slack-water bottom of the Mississippi
and across the storm-blank Iowa sky. This our dumb

hope for heaven—for every blind request, a name,
a prayer to rattle our glass-packed, backfiring hearts.

This Is What I Know about Ghosts

They are selfish.
They are books with hollow insides.

They live off memorials, steal carbon dioxide
from candles they can't even use. They

are unbidden—her in my house and only the men
could see. Him pulling my young mother back

from the wreck. They are small as a cat's plush
toy, as any real mouse. They skulk baseboards,

they squeak your car brakes. They are hungry
for your favorite shawl. In my old house,

everything woolen was ridden 'round, a hole
for every empty mouth. I threw out my sweaters

and left in the spring, told anyone who'd listen
what lives there: a ghost for the man who didn't believe

in altars, in graves, so any dead woman would do.
Her laugh a dull chime—ice cubes against glass—

when I stood in sock feet and cast my demands:
A miracle, dead woman, or show me your face.

No hands pulled me back from the wreck.
A shadow—a shuffle of wings—behind me:

drawn to the lights, when she took body
I mistook her for moths, a dozen paper bodies

in ashen heap. She wanted to be me—undone—
and then she was, as I will be.

Reading the Old News

He was your age when he disappeared,
walked to the bus stop alone and never

resurfaced. Across the river, everything
changed. He might as well have been you,

and from then we were leashed—she knew
what was out there, she knew how to

dissolve. *Our boys don't grow into men,*
and when they do, they don't last. You did,

and you wore him like a shadow, tucked
in with boys in ties. *Nobody in, nobody*

out. Wait for your sister by the iron gate.
Grandmother told her they'd find him

walled underneath some stairs. A boy
becomes a finger of dust like that. A girl

is gone faster than a boy, she knows—
clip-on ties break away when grabbed,

but ribbons and braids can tether. *Pour*
the milk, she says, her shadow flickering

the kitchen wall, ten-feet tall and watchful.
What are these childhoods free of danger,

these fairy tales un-fanged? They drag the city
for the old news, we talk across your little

girl's head. We were good and it meant
nothing. Grandmother had the sight. *Nobody*

in, nobody out, the dead boys still knocking
the plaster off walls. The computer can age him

into your gray hair. She kept looking for
what she had lost. On the street view map

I found us: the gate, the school, a man—Who
is he?—and ringing, ringing (but in whose name?)

—the bell of the saint of the day.

The Phone Only Rings When Someone Dies

> *"Did gods make the stars*
> *from the bones of dead sparrows?"*
> — *Rane Arroyo*

My cat sits at the window, hunts
the flickering bird shadows from behind
the canvas curtains. Buddhas in fur,
Rane called cats, himself a hole
in this day. The cat watches, swishes
his tail, thwaps the pane
with a clawless paw, batting the four noble truths away.

Animals are supposed to be lessons, to teach us to love
in short bursts.

I've learned to dread a beloved name
on the caller ID. Then I return the favor:
the bad news about Mark not any easier after
the bad news about Rane, after which I taught
my students the term elegy,
thought by naming it, by laying their
hands on it, I would understand
that we would not trade poems or dance moves
or gossip in the corners of parties
he'd plus-one us into
again.

                                    Thwap.

It's the sound bewildered birds make
when the curtains are open and they collide
with windows, mistaking the glass

for all the world ahead. The cat would kill them, more fodder
for stars. The birds chatter,
oblivious to my sweet, stupid cat who can't know the difference
between impression and body, and so he tries again.

                                    Thwap.
I can't tell the difference
between Mark the lion—always laughing—
and Mark who could not bear his own ton of trembling
feathers. A breeze lifts all the leaves at once—
and there go those fucking birds again,
their shadows streaking air without weight. If only
I could pull back the drapes, expose them to the light.

I could use Rane's advice.

The Bitters Shortage

That was the year the bottles didn't
fill, a plant seized, supply line choked,
our cocktails bereft. I became

undashed. Angostura, an amber code
for measured sipping, for the cutting
of syrup so sweetness won't curdle

the fickle pH of my desire. After
the bitters, what remains: the mule kick
of straight shots, the pucker of lemon

drops under the blue-ribbon moon
blinking above the bar, all deserved.
The mixologists (those mad DJs)

made their own, infusing waitress tears
with kitchen weeds, but not all
our chemistries were so tightly

under thumb. It was enough to make
my teeth ache, that muddled marriage
of sugar and fruit, and what of learned appetites

for easy drinking? It was enough to drive me
back to the debunked taste map,
where what I crave remained lodged, hard

to reach, back near the throat with all
my early warnings half-swallowed.

And yet my glass, near empty.

And yet this heart, threatening to slip
up my tongue to rest, a cherry siren,
upon the tip.

Outside Atlantic City

When Bruce Springsteen wants to get
away, he leaves behind the Stone Pony
and hides inside the wood and tin-sheeting
belly of Lucy, the six-story elephantine
colossus, a mournful Victorian fancy
guarding the coast of Margate, New Jersey.

I know this because that is where I would go
to get away from being me if I could,
though I am not even myself most days,
let alone anyone's boss, the precise state
to which Bruce Springsteen surely,
some days, aspires. It is said that elephants

have great memories, and though Lucy's
temporal lobes are velveteen cushions
stuffed with horsehair bundles, their infinite
capacity comforts him, allows him to store
his regrets in her folds, empty his wallet
for a while. Here are the papers to induct
the E Street Band into the Rock and Roll Hall of Fame,
that faltering chimera, that cafeteria of spent
guitar picks and spangle. Tucked away deep,

the boardwalk heyday. And here, in the far
reaches, "Tunnel of Love," smelling of sawdust
and stale wedding cake, bundled in faded
silk blouses. Underneath, in a deep place only
Bruce Springsteen can find, a brilliant disguise—
a gray mask with sailcloth ears and a long,

wrinkled trunk, for when he must emerge,
stumble forth into the morning sun, wiping

glitter from his blinking eyes. At a sanctuary
in Tennessee, two elephants reunited after
twenty years apart nearly break down a steel gate
to wrap their trunks tighter around each other.

What does Bruce Springsteen hold tight?
Bruce, we each have our own beast belly,
own at least one shabby disguise. We know
you and we can see you because
we are all hiding in plain sight.

Turn the Dial Volvelle

The elephant's agony eye
beams a lighthouse
welcome warning

That girl in patent shoes
shreds a program
into nothing

One banjo left for dead
holds ten thousand
oh my darlings

House keys in the box
are a mix tape's
counter-charming

My ring flipped to the sky
waits for small hands
fortune hunting

The jukebox lit for play
might regret its choice
come morning

A lily dressed in white
keeps the bedside
candle burning

The coaster claimed by sea
seats two per car
no jumping

Souvenir

In Lithuania, close to the Latvian border, crosses
on a hill yawn their arms wide, so many
stiff hugs—you might stumble upon a confession
received in their shadows. You might give yours.
What do you have to say for yourself? It is not clear

who hangs the beaded rosaries on iron bars to clink
in the wind, strange music. Some medieval obsessions
survive. Someone will forgive you. In Père Lachaise,
Oscar Wilde's pilgrims leave behind scarlet kisses,
confessions to his tomb. There was a man, scarved

and drawn, searching for Maria Callas. I had the map.
Who did I love? In Montparnasse, I left behind a torn
ticket for Serge Gainsbourg. In New York, I was in
the right place at the right time, outside the Apollo
for James Brown's wake, inching up 125th Street after

five freezing hours to see his perfect wig, his cobalt suit,
a stage so small in person. I left behind a marriage,
tucked in a gilded casket where it belonged. The wrong
woman in the wrong place—broken clocks,
their lucky strikes—Someone might forgive me. I could

have used a confession. I wrote mine on the wall
around Graceland, small as a link in a rosary's chain.
I would play a game of chance. In Memphis, I tossed
a ring at the highest tier of a fountain. Gleaming arc—
it landed in the water, clinking all the penny wishes.

A Physics Experiment

Dusk hits my untidy street and two scrawny boys
on bikes glide into
coming traffic, playing chicken
against Toyotas, those eternal
shaggy haircuts shielding
squinting eyes from setting
sun. I honk and shout

but they will not be deterred.
Would you? These same boys
will spring like dandelions
from every cracked sidewalk
until the sun supernovas or
skateboards vanish, whichever
comes first. They haven't yet

approached the simmering pack
of roving girls who tremble
with the terrible secrets
of fourteen—there's time for that
when they trade stickered decks
for fastbacks, idle evenings
for overtime at the Dairy Kastle.

For now, most of what they know are empty
pillows left cool in the wake
of swing-shift moms, those wild
hours between microwaved
dinners and dad's last call when

spring wind whips them
through flickering streetlamps:
elegant as baby deer, all legs
and giant eyes, flirting with my rushing
headlights, beautiful in their refusal,
so I swerve first.

Star Jet Standing

It begins with a hurricane sweeping Seaside Heights
onto the ocean floor. Yards out in the surf—
a fossil of the shattered boardwalk—the roller coaster,
as much a museum centerpiece as any mammoth
or T. rex bones. Rebuilding is a dubious art,
what with the uncertain rate of rust, but Bruce Springsteen

rolls up his pants, eyeballs the Star Jet
from a power stance on the beach: it's night
and the boardwalk unnaturally dark. The ocean
roars, a cover for his cause. Maybe it's playing

to the back of the room, to the boys desperate
for a gesture, but turning back is not
an option. He grips the casing, rattles
the skeleton as waves crash the tops of his boots,
the fine Atlantic salt crusting his cuffs,
up to his knees, every drop fountained
into the higher truth of the winter night sky.
A saxophone solo is what this mission needs,

he thinks like always since the Big Man died:
like he couldn't use a boost up a mountain shoulder,
like he couldn't use another set
of hands to tie the bandana around his head, kiss him
gently as a father? And this is how we separate
the boys from the men, these a cappella solos?
It's one hand on top of the other
and the slow rush of blood to his feet and
the mysterious black of the sea before him.

Bruce Springsteen pauses halfway up—

a car, intact but creaking. He kneels
in the fragile seat and wonders if this could be
a reasonable way to die, to rattle loose
from the tether until the sudden
overtakes him, a fitting map
to the flattened world.
Spit takes the long way down.
The joists clatter under rickety tracks.
Soon the Coast Guard will be back. The wind has picked up.
A dog left behind howls a harmonica cantata,
and Bruce Springsteen thinks

that'll have to do. Footfalls on steel
are a rhythm section, the flag furled in his back pocket
where a heart-red hat once flamed. It ends

at the summit, this swaying land claimed
for everything that dies and someday comes back,
and here is the proof: he can almost see
Atlantic City from here, planting the flag
in silhouette against the moon, claiming the coaster
as sovereign nation until the spotlight sweeping,
the boat horn barking, and Bruce Springsteen making
himself

a reed, a sapling, anything that can bend into the night
and come out tall by morning.

PART TWO

Looking for Tea Leaves in Dry Glasses

"There is no scientific evidence that the future
can be determined through
interpretation of these patterns."
—Wikipedia

My zipper has a mind
of its own. These narrow freckled
shoulders can't keep satin straps

from slipping down, further
down, but nobody's watching.
My ears buzz harp and pedal steel,

lips hum a bourbon honeybee sting
but at the glass bottom, no fortune.
I fix bedtime tea like a good girl

and the grounds remind me
oh, that time won't wait. Once I tore
a cabin down with one wink, those nights

filled with impressing on my back
the bark of a thousand anonymous
trees. Chestnut burrs prickled

my bare, curved insole, so pink
in flush. The earned sweat of our taut
stomachs fed a thousand creeks,

spawned mosquitoes who sucked
our blood and we allowed it. It didn't
last. I need a next move. I am overgrown

back to wild, with forgiveness my skin's
only story—left with mother-of-pearl
puddles shimmering on pay-at-the-pump,

tiny furrows feathering my eyes, a future
I'd rather not cull from my palm, these stones,
the determination of lucky and unlucky days.

Crash Course: Geology

My craggy semi-precious, find something else
to not get over for a while. Describe how want
gleams like quartz through the sediment of all those
sad legends, as I pocket river stones to polish
for my report. Everyone dies, we learn so early—

I lecture myself, too. Soft bodies reach a limit.
Our igneous, irregular hearts born of fire, cooled
to solid and labeled. I will make another if you
light the flame. When did my dreams get so small?
Explain depth, how I am covered by a layer
of the ground you walk, how it swings in a vial
around my neck. This test (like you) an open book,
dragging my finger, mouthing the words *I may not
pass.* Thrown back into the volcano, I am forging

a new story as you stand on the lip and wave,
a mirage, a canceled postmark, a tectonic
shift. I wouldn't know a glacial change if I saw one.
No time for tumbled polish—I'm carving fuel
from fossil. Marl to marble, shale to slate, a story pressed
between foliated lines, this bloodroot, my vein of clay.

Like Pine Barrens Dark

Hours creep by in the ladder stand, scraping
like a blade sharpening on stone.

This is the hour of the wolf.
Bruce Springsteen has gone hunting.

He knows he is not a slayer, only
that he lives in New Jersey, where weird
is just another chili-dog day
at the beach. But lately
dogs have gone missing.
A shadow falls across the golf course.
Blink and you'll miss it, but you swear
you saw a long, forked tail. Wings.
And then, there is the empty
Toyota parked off a dirt road, top peeled
back like a sardine can, six-pack
still cold on the seat.

There is more than one way to be
a hero. Bruce Springsteen's eyes adjust
to the charcoal dark. *Blood is only
blood*, he tells himself—half mantra,
half plea.

You don't have to be a big man
to bring a demon down, but what
urine baptism does a monster hunt
demand? Pennsylvania deer won't prepare

you for this, this rough beast
and its camel-domed head.

Bruce Springsteen thinks he should star
in his own comics—thighs pumped-
up near bursting through trousers,
a hammer in one hand, rail spike
above head. Or a samurai spinoff:
Ronin with a six-string, an epic
vengeance tale. He smacks his face
lightly, a reminder to listen
for cloven hooves upon ground,
a shriek too weird
to be wind.

He will wait, and when it swoops
down to crush him in jaw, wailing,
Bruce Springsteen will be ready
to cowboy himself
upon its back, to mount it
like an electric bull,
grab hold of those devil leather wings
and *ride, baby, ride*.

Listening to Queen in Mickey's Pub

What I like best tonight: the jukebox
absorbs my voice into Freddie's and we are
one. Crackling billiards, the eight ball ricochets

hypotenuse-up into a perfect right
angle, and I am experimenting with what
can fit inside a chalk cube's low blue

dent. A theorem to determine
what the heart can bear? Tender
of the bar, this rough angel cradles

St. Jude in the hollow of her neck,
loads a tray with our round, palms
my elbow: how to balance the world

with my wrist. I'll learn, I promise,
flashbulb eyes exploding: I could master
one smooth move, the slow-clap and

medal kind, a theory to believe in
even if I can't see it, like the Big Bang,
this weight of nothing in my hand.

Pilgrimage: Nashville to Memphis

Nothing is certain anymore
except bruised thighs banged against tables:
back porch bent notes, so familiar
after a year such as this. Driving deep
into country, nothing can stop this

persistent throb, thrumming like
our feet to the music, remembering
original heartbreak: our stumbling
fathers, those first lost loves.
We have left
the pews of Ryman for the untold
wilds of Beale, traded fringe
for dirty choir robes
and a sequined future gleaming. Tangled

in kudzu, utility poles form living crosses,
redemption just around the bend—
I dreamed we drifted to the end

of an interstate lane, but rather than merging
the road dropped, guardrail unable
to save us and we fell, gathering
speed until the inevitable:
drenched, startled waking.

Dominique throws back
her head, roars wild at the sky—its threat
to crack open an empty fist.

With her in the back, we can go
anywhere: our courage lives

in the hollow of her throat.
Jeffrey, our heart, knuckles
the wheel, homesick but smiling,
determined to love the world
if it kills him. And me—I'm tracing red

highway lines with a scarred, ringless finger.
Hoping I'm steering
us right, I count roadkill
raccoons slumped on the shoulder—one-two-three,
lost turtles shocked, frozen in shells
between uneven lanes.

Break-Up Takeout

The fortune cookie gloats: *Stop searching*
forever. Happiness is just next to you, as if

cartons of Buddha's Delight, infinitely meatless,
could know me so well. Spring rain rushes

all my sins down marked storm drains, stenciled
fish imploring: *no poison*. I will try.

I will fail. I will fall, skidding palms rough
on the slick black street. Gravel-torn skin,

I'm knocked out of my shoes, a dank
river smell around me, on me,

every primordial bit soaking my jeans.
What if we climbed from the swamps and this

is all I did with Eden: pairing red wine
with Thin Mints, stumbling from bar

to backyard, raccooning through trash
for tea leaves to read back in tongues?

Forgive me. Forget fortune, my song.

Down-and-Out in Beatersville

Bruce Springsteen and Morgan Freeman—
which is to say, Scooter and God, glorious
in his most recent cinematic-resonant
incarnation—walk into a bar. Let us say
this bar is in Aspen and they are promoting a film.
Bruce Springsteen is concerned about the creeping

darkness, what it can do to a man's heart and
the lines around his woman's eyes, plus he has
a bone to pick about the noise level on his street,
the afterhours racers he tries so desperately
to love—he sets hymns for them to heartbreaking
guitar in spite of the uncharitable thoughts

he attributes grudgingly to his advancing age, a tactic
Morgan Freeman approves, expansive love
being, generally speaking, what the representational
He is all about. The word of the day is despair,
and what Bruce Springsteen might could do for a solid

eight hours without the throaty growl of a Mach Shorty
dragging through his dreams. He is open to suggestions.
He worries he might be overcompensating, and then he
worries
he might be atoning for some past sin, someone's girl
into whose eyes he planted a haunted

look. The bartender, who does not fancy himself
a priest, pours Freeman the usual—sweet vermouth

on the rocks, while Bruce shreds the cocktail napkin,
damp under his bottle. And what of the new wise
dude on the scene, Freeman wonders, of the beatific
wunderkind who made all the press agents swoon?
What tricks, from up which sleeve, might he pull?

Back to the darkness and its creeping borders, but
Freeman holds one finger to Bruce Springsteen's
mouth and offers to arm wrestle him for it. For what?
Forgiveness, says Morgan Freeman, checking his phone
for a text from his agent, or *to know finally the embrace
of my filmic love*, or—and here he pauses in that way
that suggests: whichever comes first, for he is also,
you might have heard, a man who can get things
for you—*a good night's sleep.*

Tinnitus Valentine

The ringing in my ear: the sound
nerves make when they die. Summer-
sweet buzz—my dried, pressed violet,
my constant catastrophe, a reminder
of too-loud speakers and no foam
plugs. No doctors—I prefer to be
the keeper of the chart of my own
flaws. So many lessons not to learn:
Come to Jesus, come in-to Jee-zus!
the man in his anonymous overcoat
sings on the corner of Wabash,
and still the crickets in my head.
Memento mori, the roar in my stomach
when you kiss me lives here.
I will raise my voice rather than lose
this prayer chime, this fading
stamp on my hand.

Mother Says Dead Boys Live in the Old Kitchen

cooking up ways to remind us: they are

our kin. I dare you to knock and run.
Dare you to knock and stay. Silvered

portraits, fist upon chin: appraise. One
cousin a murderer not yet crossed

over, but ask his daddy how: one cousin
killed and guess who married his sister,

fists full of rice and a fluttering veil?
What does that make the rest of us?

Even me? Here, a mottled mirror.
Mutter a name to that mirror three times,

and who will come to save me, cousin
Beau, a Carmen Miranda painting,

a scarf, a convertible legacy? A likely story.
O, you cousins twice-removed: shy voice

drowned by oncoming trains, crumpled
trunk of a body that could not grow,

mushroom unearthed in an album's vellum.
And you unnamed cousins, crowding

the ambrosia barbecues, jostling clumsy
unbaptized graves. I believe I believe I saw

old news written on the fogged-up window.
I believe we are in debt, and we owe

at least one boy back. Yes,
this is my cousin: a number, a story, a case.

When you sing into the kitchen,
into the news, the wind whistles back: the dead

boys live in the old kitchen. Why else
the padlock, the bar across the door?

The dead boys are cooking up breakfast,
warming their hands on steaming mugs.

My dead boy, if you're not dead now,
you will be soon.

Another Heaven on Earth

St. Edna groans through drafty stone:
the rain is full of ghosts tonight, sweet
antifreeze an alley dog's last treat.
Outbound train, an ashen crumble,
a vague unease: a misheard scrap, a twist of lips
whistling me awake.

How should I go on from here, to place
my feet in order? Heels, toes. Every day,

skin cells flake, fall, only to be
replaced. The motes in the smart dust
will find the light before my eyes
tremble open, before I fumble my glasses,
before the alarm's last grace
scatters a threadbare dream.

Give us this day our shambled commute,
our bagels wrapped in wax.

To my mother, I say: *Will call you later
okay?* And I don't.

To my student, I write: *Death is an actor
who does his own stunts.*

Surrounded by everything that ever was,
my pockets, too, are never quite empty:
I pack my dead around, those little mice—
slip my fingers in and fondle their heads
like beads. They clamor, squeaking prayers,
growing fat on the crumbs of all that I waste.

My Notes on Entomology Lab Procedure

Curl inward, become a log. Summer is best
when it's warm and you have nothing
but time. Grow a thick, shaggy bark,
let water stand in
your grooves. Allow what will
collect under you to burrow.

                                   Forget
flashlights, forget camping lanterns
casting shadows across the needled
ground. As the moon fingernails,
roll over, let the night air shock
their legs in mid-squirm. In the near-dark,
shake those secrets out, roll
them into pellets, and scatter like grain.

You're still human, no matter what
you're to do—to collect the bug,
you must see like the bug. For aphids, look
for bite holes in the leaves of a full green plant,
for signs of hunger. Pose nearby: anemone
your fingers like fronds. The breeze
will stir you. Sway as though
it is way past lunchtime, then snap

while they feed.
                      To catch a cricket,
crouch in the knee-high grasses
of the back half-acre, rub your calf
gently across your shin. Squeak

and jump. Squeak and jump. Land,
and when we all shake loose, it's tiny
fireworks above the wheaten tips,
the first kiss from a boy who will
betray you.

       Remember the last
grotesque human replica you saw—
parade balloon, cigar-store Indian—
how you started before adjusting
to the unreal face? In the gasping
moment, the dummy's advantage.

The dummy, in this case, is you.

To attract a dragonfly, turn on the radio.
Find fireflies by making out in the dark.
For a wasp, offer a single bare arm.
A fly, last week's plum. A moth, cover
your mirrors with black muslin, light
candles in every corner of your house.

You won't have to go looking for a roach.
The roach will come looking for you.

Here is a mason jar with no breath-holes,
no grass lining. Don't look away.
Cyanide from a post office box. Layer
sawdust on plaster of Paris. Sweet,
dry chamber. A funeral home's cry
room, a silk flower factory. A few tears
and your poison is active, your kill

ajar. You have your black velvet,
your straight pins, your precise, hand-
lettered labels. You have your shoulders
swelling under your shirt, a locust rattling
inside your chest, the room fractaling
right before your eyes.

Schnitzelburg in Flames

Or the camelback on the corner ignites:
whoosh—a meth lab sets the block aglow.
Another night, another end of the world—
barely worth mentioning, like the stinging
ammonia we all pretended not to smell.
What else can we ignore away? We are
walking disasters, living tap to mouth
at the bar named after our neighbors.
Days like this, every one of my scars twitch—
fused seams humming my skin's own
secret language. *It will rain in a bit*
is their promise, and my joints agree,
sparks shooting from my knuckles,
waiting (like so many of us are) to explode.

Decomposition Studies

When he goes, Bruce Springsteen declares
one night over dinner, let him go
to the body farm—compost unburied
somewhere on two acres of bloodroot,
witch hazel, carpet of leaves. Let him be
useful, he mumbles over tacos,
never mind that he's not mountain-born,
that salt water won't rust his belt buckle
down. He wants to train dogs to find

those gone missing with the memory
of moldering ruin when they hunt—
because a body should know how to be
found. If undone is what we already are,
let us clasp our hands: holy horsefly,
maggot, wasp. Bruce Springsteen
knows if you sing backup for a body
on a resurrection song, you are open to

certain ideas beyond Cleveland, Memphis,
beyond Viking ship fossils and boots, still
life with ball cap, a life-sized wax doll.
Bruce Springsteen is aware of the finite
lease, of nitrogen and a dramatic change
in pH. A body gets dangerous in a shallow
grave. A body gets eaten so many odd
ways, a smile stretches up through
the beetles. The dogs recognize

the breakdown is everything. But where will we
lay our guitar picks in tribute, our silk flower
wreaths on Memorial Day? Bruce Springsteen says
leave only footprints, and a rotting arm.
A body should know how to find its father.
A dog can be trained to hunt. Everything

changes: the wonderful and awful truth.
Keep your trash, little girl, your candlewax
weeping, your match light winked out
by the dew. Pick up a leaf, red as
bandana, press it in wind-rattled pages.

Don't apologize for your live nerves.
Carve your name on the face of the mountain.
Pocket a rock mistaken for bone.

Alphabetizing Your Records

Here comes the season of old loves
plopping from trees like rotten
fruit, past ripe, sweet ambush
of slip and squish, everywhere,
from the fish fry to the inbox:
heartbreakers and unrequiteds,
thicker now but down to a one,

smiling. The word of the day
is *undulant*. Honeysuckle's
strong scent rushing the park
like the crushing young hustlers
slinking its edges, like the crisp
mint of a drummer's wild curls,
like everything else you have

to smell close, deep to believe.
Shock. The act of the day is
replacement. To pull steady,
gently firm, the day a broken
needle popped off a cartridge.
Waiting for the click, you blow
dust from a found record, no

more hiss. Tiny mouth collector,
this is the season of catch and
release, stray cats scratching
your door. What could you find
inside an old sleeve? A tin bird
chorus, ravenous, opened wide.
Soon, we enter the season of *please*.

Las Meninas

—after the painting by Velázquez

And there stands the Infanta Margarita—
the ugly daughter—a loose translation
but certain as baroque panel dresses,
as the mastiff at the feet of the fool. *My joy*,
the king calls her in his letters. *A diamond*
for my joy, for my brother's new wife.
Things were different in those days, rough
for a Habsburg girl, all your inbred
flaws rendered in exquisite, theological
detail. Oof,—that forehead. But her father

loves her. He gave her a diamond,
a fancy gray-blue number like
the Hope, now cut and recut until
culture itself curled up and died, sh-boom.
What do we lose with the flaws, anyway?
And oh, those lesser maids—little beauties
uncertain of their fathers, catching
the edges of Margarita's holy light.

It's a living. There will be studies. Always
more portraits, artists—*Hello, hello again*.

Over my friend's desk, a clown-
handed stick figure labeled *DAD!*,
shock-topped stick kids pogo-ing
around him. The physics are shaky,
but the smiles could cut glass.
Trust me, little maid, if you can—

your father, he loves you
and this is not a dream, though you are
still not the last Habsburg, only
a girl in first or second grade.
What war could she wage
in that dress, anyway? It is time for
Easter Mass, *sh-boom*. Assemble

the maids. My father's letters are formal
but he loved me, and he died—*Hello,*
hello again, little maid, little fool, my only
medal a diamond gleaming red on my chest.

Violet Hour at the Oak Street Lounge

As if we didn't already know from so long
sitting in this bar that everything beautiful
fades, you point out a hole in the shirt

I just admired, which you rescued from
a thrift store bin. A friend is in love and
he couldn't have been happier to sit in rush-

hour traffic to tell me. I wanted to tell him
hungry moths have chomped my best wool,
and soft cotton will wear thin, revealing

the weave of threads—a stuttering cross-
hatch, the frost pattern on a windshield—
before breaking apart, cauterizing ends

to form a circle: small at first, but rippling
out each time you push a fingertip against
the lip of the hole, tasting resistance. Add

that to all we know: your case-less pillow,
my busted banjo eyes. I wish him charms
to ward off the rot: cedar chips, dry cleaning,

humidifiers. I wish his far-off sweet girl
sleepless nights, but the good kind. I wish
a fresh twin of your shirt—same gentle riot

of orange blooms—to materialize for you
at the Goodwill racks. A dead ringer,
your replacement: bright, whole, ready to wear.

PART THREE

The Dream and What Follows

On certain days when spring,
crippled, doesn't quite make good
on its wild promise, nothing's more
aching than how, in "Prove It All Night,"
Bruce Springsteen drawls out
the vowel in "dream"—*draym*, he says—
to rhyme with *pain* and *ain't*, a subtle
yet effective nod to what I believe
to be the trinity of Bruce—a clenched

doxology in which the high-speed collision
of the second and third into the first
forge the only granted rebirths.
In that *draym* I feel like he is nearly
Southern, that elastic diphthong stinking
of creekwater behind his uncle's garage,
dipping like a fraying rope swing
into the green that swallows all
muttered prayers, even his.

Confession:
I did not love Bruce Springsteen until
I turned thirty and set my own home on fire,
walked away from the ashes and looked
my declining self in the face. Like love,
Bruce is wasted on the young. *You may be a little old,*
but I will still fuck you, Bruce says, and that was a tough sell
to the me who once thought all I'd ever need
is Thai food and a degree from a nice college.
How I lied to myself: pretending

those staggering piano chords did not play
for me but for the long hauls back home,
the factory floor malcontents, the county queen
now fallen in her checkered kitchen and more
beautiful to me than ever.
But if everything that dies
finally winds its way back, what of the *Born to Run* axiom
that speed plus distance defeats time?

I got a scenic route tattooed up that long soft drag
between my elbow and my wrist. I got a sketch
of "Thunder Road" burning a hole in my skin
with a heat that's getting hard, so hard to resist.

I got all your facts,
Bruce, learned real good right now:
when we come from nowhere, eventually
we return, pulled back for funerals, for lovers,
born with nothing but a map to the roiling spot
where all the rivers meet, its legend buried in liner notes,
in old notebooks we never thought we'd need to keep.

Inside the Oyster

Let's stay in tonight,
cook dinner in shades of pale:
champagne, baguette. Let's

get slimy. Wiggle snails
back into their shells, stuff
butter and garlic. I will deal

with the oysters. Watch me
grip this craggy, clamped
mouth, force knife between lips

until a litany pours out,
a lovers' quarrel that smells
like the sea. Tell me you don't

mind a little violence. Tell me
you're not afraid of brine. My
hand a barnacled hull, yours

a tilled garden. The escargot
bubble over, a steaming
suburb—promise that will never

be us. And look, inside, what
I found: a pea crab waving
it spindly arms, a slow

salute to second chances.
Some gifts surface without
warning: one creature alive

inside another, a bonus pearl
to pop with your blessed
tongue, oh salty, sweet surprise.

The Living Dead

We went away to Pittsburgh for a lovers'
weekend, which, really, was weird enough,

drove out to the cemetery in the opening
scene of Romero's *Night of the Living Dead*—

horror pilgrims, *wish-you-were-heres* with
bloody postmarks. I love you like zombies

love bad movies, and I would follow
a sarcophagus fly across the stylish Alps

to guest-star in your fevered prog-rock
dreams, so we find the stone where Barbra

caught herself and Johnny went down
fighting—they wanted to visit their father's

grave. I have never visited mine,
nearly thirty years tamped, but someday you'll slip

your hand in mine on an exotic
trip to Long Island, and we will stand

in the shadow of his stone-faced angel,
we will soak the soil with Guinness

and wail a sea shanty: *What do you do
with a drunken sailor, so earl-aye in the morning?*

Take him to breakfast, let him meet
my love? He is dead and this is a dream

and the fly cannot know my heart. When he
reanimates, will you whisper a prayer, steady

my aim for the bulls-eye brow—oh, that cross
of ash and dirt, the *X* that marks the living spot?

On Who Made the First Move

Our second skins soaked, thin cotton
clinging to chests thrilled with each
silent jab of lightning, there we were

on the edge of leaf-heavy summer,
storm crashing like an anvil dangled

by one slim thread above a cartoon
sidewalk, struck dumb in thrall, ink
spreading our names across the sky—

Wait, it happened like this: cool dark
of the beer cave, so many turncoat

soldiers lined against a wall, nervous
laugh at the door's click, quite final,
as if thirst could be this illicit, as if

they wouldn't find us come morning,
icicled mouths frozen scant inches

from their marks—Look, no, let me
try again: loose embers Morse code
secrets all around us, charcoal seeping

into flyaway hair, stinging citronella
eyes—What can it mean at the end

of such a season—what we read into,
what is left behind? Tell me before I

write it down wrong, drenched before

we knew it was raining, preserved
in place, still sitting in this spot,

waiting for nothing and everything to begin.

Give Me a Room, I Will Make of It Something

Like this hole in the floor—
it's a mail slot for delivering messages
to my doppelganger. It's a portal
to another dimension in which I
and everyone I know are made
of balsa wood and held together
with glue. It is not so far
from the truth. It is a wound
in the heart of the building. It is
a window into my level self, a fissure
with edges rubbed fine from sand.
It is a wormhole. Stay back; it is
not a slide.

In the second room, the gallery
of repetitive vision, on the floor,
the wall, are the spots I see
when I close my eyes, hold
my breath. The spots of hope
and of dread. In the mirrors stare
their multiplied faces.
Notice how this room
reminds me of the roller rink
on disco night. Notice how
we all remove our shoes,
but are given no skates
in return.

Past mirrors and doors
are more mirrors and more

red-hot dots and posing
beauties waiting for someone gently
to un-pose them. Up the tilted ramp.

Now the dark room: two chairs, two
people. We cannot see
the tips of our fingers. Not soothing.
Others are trying
to get in, but there is only room
for two. Maybe it has been two
minutes, maybe five. I can't wait.
I back out of the room to the red box pulsing
and here are the speakers of my stereo.

Covered in crimson, twin suns setting
in the fine dust of the atmosphere
on a planet just this unlike our own.
Thumping, rusty hearts left wet
too long under dual suns. They speak
a language faintly like German, tinged
with gutted fairy tales, with Black
Forest cherries, with corrosion,
with the march down the bed
of the river. Then the rushing,
the diving, the thunderous water below.

This Is Not a Poem about Bruce Springsteen

This is a poem about
Vic Chesnutt and how I wish
his songs played behind
those mustaches reading Civil War
letters to beloveds back home
in filmstrips and how little like
"When Johnny Comes Marching Home"
a border state really sounds.

This is also a poem about
Buddy Holly, his hiccups
giving voice to a particular,
exquisite set of pins
and high-school needles. This is
a poem about Jeff Buckley
and the swaying bridge
I eyeballed one night,
trusting neither my balance
nor my swimming chops.

Memphis: I will pay your debt
someday. A highway exit three hours
south and a riot of dogwoods
remind me. Somehow, this is
a poem about Elliott Smith,
which is to say this is a poem
for Vic Chesnutt's legs and
the hubcap–hall pass chained
to them, for the battlefield map
and the cool spot underneath

my flaming cheek. This is not
a poem about Bruce Springsteen,
but I suppose, like all of them,
it might as well be.

A Literature Exam

I.

You say *Wasteland*, I say *April*.

Wasteland!
                    April!
Wasteland!
                    April!

Our sneakered feet thudding the blacktop,
neon braided rope swished above our heads,
slicing the blossom-choked air.
                                Your arms are full,
your hair is wet / your momma got captured
                                in a butterfly net

One / two / three / four / fasterfasterfaster / trip

Our dribbling echoed *jug/jug*, our handclaps
flinted twit/twit. We opened the barn door
and kicked out the hay, we flashlit
bunk beds waiting for the late frost
to pass until our plastic barretted–braids
could clack in time with our jumping,
gunfire like jacks against themselves.

Red, red rocks
all sharp and tall
                    cast your shadow
                    on the wailing wall

In the beams of the bridge, what we didn't know: children
our age buried. What we couldn't catch:
plague dreams curtsying like ashes
around our heads.

                Double double / father father
double double / blue blue

And then it was over, a father
undone, a red in the morning rest,

                    and me the hyacinth girl askew—
a root tangle, a rats' alley trailing my heaving chest.

II.

In April the ground thaws like a roast.

Every part of me smells like the river
because I have never lived anywhere
but on the banks of a river. Fast forward: the lock

lifts all boats in spite of themselves, crumpled
wallet photos floating in the wake, outboard
motor chortling

      he who was living / is now dead
   he who was living / is now dead

The sky kisses, as I once did,
sweet you, the gasoline surface of the lake,
another predictable ending.

They say you cannot roll in your own-
made mess, but what of lessons you can't
unlearn, a boundless patience unwrapped?

A revolver shot in the Pennsylvania silence.
A ninja star fired through a beer-can belly.

Every story ends with a failing heart.

Ci-ca-da Sy-ca-more's /
            stac-ca-to stutter
Took her to the dance /
            but left with another

I must go back to the schoolyard—
to the piked iron gate, the Catholic brown
and yellow wool. Come. We must go back

past rusted tetherball and the goose guarding,
black widows swarming a rental stoop, back
to trick-bottom suitcases, fur stoles, and the cops
(another way of saying my father was a thief),
those hollow insides stuffed with the stories
I'll tell myself in verse, or else in ruin.

Summer Prayer

As a kid, I read up on constellations,
studied the night sky with naked eyes
and a map I dug from the dusty depths
of my breakfast cereal box, straining
to connect the granular dots into shapes

more like animal crackers than Cheerios,
wondering how Polaris, that Mayan
monkey head, morphed into a Bedouin
billy goat, then became a little dipper,
and then, simply, finally, a lesser bear.

Now I know that wine turns sour
not when Sirius raises one furred
eyebrow at gushing fire hydrants but
when baked too long in the ovens of
orange recycling bins. What will I do

with the dog days left me? Let us walk
our canoe through the shallows, river
so dry we can't paddle, scraping
metal on rocks shifting fast under our
feet. Let us light the citronella against

mosquitoes, count homemade acetylene
bomb explosions in the cul-de-sac cookout
cheer. And when the smoke clears, let me
count pinprick freckles clustered near
the hinge of your knee, let me name them

after all our lousy miracles unbound. Look,
this one's *Darkness on the Edge of Town*,
this is Gold Rush eucalyptus, shelter cat,
moonbow, Mennonite girls rollerblading
the beach. Connect them and they form

a rough, rounded question mark, like
a 1962 Karmann Ghia or a single white,
paper sky-lantern, powered by candle
and burning wish, released into the stars
to mingle: our hopeful, rising debris.

It's Hard to Be the Boss in the Capital City

I. The WWII Memorial

They say the wall that mirrors is toughest,
but nobody warned him about the white
stone, states echoing dates with two oceans
between them. Bruce Springsteen fears
the eyes of the world are upon him, blinking
away their sleep. Delaware, New Jersey, Kentucky,
Maine. The internet doctor
diagnosed him—paranoid (only a little misspelled!),

a harmless quirk, those luxuries of peace.
The capital's efficiency spooks him, how
they turn choked water into gazing pools,
little signs begging no chip-in coins, though
he can count the penny wishes on more
than one hand. Vermont, Mississippi,
Minnesota, Kansas. A lone plastic flower
browns in the sun. Bruce Springsteen met
Tom Hanks once—the Oscars—nice guy,
makes those films he watches

when he can't sleep. The decision to attack
at this time and place will be based on the best
information available. Bruce Springsteen
licks a finger to test the rough surface.
Alsace, Rhineland, Guadalcanal
bloom like fever under his tongue.
He looks both ways, then, under a dead man's
hat, scratches "Forgive All" into the stone.

II. The Reflective Pool

His task not an easy one: to slip
the tour guide's righteous eye and march
straight into their waters. What else
are they here for, if not to wet a man's hair down?
We must be ready to dare. It is Thanksgiving,
the mall is quiet, resting its glories under
waning sun.

It is time—

the decision to attack at this time and place
will be based on the best information available.
Bruce Springsteen
dips a finger to test the November pool,
then like a flash, like the last bass whipping
on a line in the pinkest dawn, he is winking
under the water. The camera phones open.
Let the tubes say their prayers,
a witness choir of likes and ugly thoughts.
This is his body and this his blood, this
tepid water so foreign for fall, this meager
twenty-four-hour inheritance.

Let it be worth the penance of talk show rounds,
he thinks as he holds his breath underwater,
sending Mayday bubbles to the surface
in code, the simple long and short of it all.

III. The Washington Monument

Nearby, a whole museum to honor
what Icarus couldn't pull off—*but no
love for the foot-bound of us all*,
Bruce Springsteen thinks, the apes
in you and me kept in a whole other house,
their little fires and rough tools that couldn't
win a war you'd want to fight. The hopes

and prayers of liberty-loving people
wrangling shrill suburban kids
through the zoological gardens of the dead
light the way, the father of them all: a finger accusing
the sky and what lives there. The decision
to attack at this time and place will be based

on the best information available. Bruce Springsteen
licks a finger to test the fickle wind, notes the red
leaking across the horizon. Nobody notices
the clamps on his boots, the belt of picks
at the base of five hundred and fifty-
five feet and change of America's pure product.

Once, on a European tour, Bruce Springsteen
visited the cathedral in Cologne, to test
the choir loft in all its medieval glory, and saw a ciga-
rette
floating in a holy water basin at the door. *At least
a reliquary is honest*, he thinks as he climbs,
a small crowd gathering at the base.

Soon,
the jets will come in formation, radio barking
his coordinates to the feds. The color has faded
from the sky. Soon, soon, he will be at the top
of the spire of our great experiment, and what
will he see? Whose three fingers pointing back?

Life in the Flight Path

Takeoffs are noisier than landings, we learn,
barely noticing approaching planes

rumbling low through the white noise hours
before dawn. The birds have learned to leave

the tops of trees during a lumbering ascent,
returning when the wake clears to roost.

I still don't know their names; they're brown,
some gray—whatever, I don't get attached.

We learn to stop talking
when a big jet pulls in,
dialogue stuttered
with syncopated rests, a dialect wholly

our own. People take off during waking
hours, arrive near to us unbidden. So many

things move while we sleep: our Snuggies,
our steak knives, those artifacts we will

bury and buy again. Are we listening to the future
or the past? We fed the birds, now they'll

never leave. We wrap ourselves in the rhythm
of the sky as long as the planes, all safe, still fly.

★

ACKNOWLEDGMENTS

A hearty thanks to the editors of the following journals who have published these poems, some with different titles:

Barrelhouse: "Star Jet Standing"

The Collagist: "The Living Dead"

Exit 7: "My Notes on Entomology Lab Procedure"

Forklift, Ohio: "The Dream and What Follows"

The Louisville Review: "This Is What I Know about Ghosts"

The Lumberyard: "Outside Atlantic City," "Schnitzelburg in Flames"

MOTIF: Chance: "A Chemistry Exam Cheat Sheet"

MOTIF: Writing by Ear: "Break-Up Takeout"

Open 24 Hours: "On Who Made the First Move"

PANK: "Give Me a Room, I Will Make of It Something," "Mother Says Dead Boys Live in the Old Kitchen"

Pinwheel: "Decomposition Studies," "Las Meninas," "A Supermarket in New Jersey"

Redivider: "Tinnitus Valentine"

Shape of a Box: "Listening to Queen in Mickey's Pub"

Sou'wester: "Alphabetizing Your Records," "West Kentucky Heartbreak"

Verse Wisconsin: "Violet Hour in the Oak Street Lounge," "A Physics Experiment," "Souvenir"

Small Batch: A Bourbon Poetry Anthology: "Looking for Tea Leaves in Dry Glasses"

Thanks also to friends who encouraged these poems in person and in spirit: Lindsey Alexander and Jen Woods, Pam Steele, Beth Newberry, Jeffrey Lee Puckett, Niki King, Marianne Worthington, Darnell Arnoult, Jamieson Ridenhour, Amy Miller, Laura Morton, Dana McMahan, Jaki Watson, Marci Rae Johnson, Tania Runyan, Jonathan Weinert, Amy Clark. Rane Arroyo and Mark Russell Brown, you are missed.

ABOUT THE AUTHOR

photo by Drew Zipp

Erin Keane is the author of two previous books: *The Gravity Soundtrack* (WordFarm, 2007) and *Death-Defying Acts* (WordFarm, 2010), a novel in poems about the circus and finalist for the *Foreword Book of the Year*. She's an arts reporter and critic in Louisville, Kentucky, where she works for an NPR affiliate and produces the short fiction radio show *Unbound*. Keane lives under the flight path, near a secret cemetery. She'd be happy to show you around.

Other titles available by this author:

The Gravity Soundtrack
Death-Defying Acts

Additional resources by/about this author:

Unbound short fiction radio show
http://wfpl.org/programs/unbound

arts reporting
http://wfpl.org/people/erin-keane

website
http://www.sensilla.com/

★

★

★

www.ingramcontent.com/pod-product-compliance
Lightning Source LLC
Chambersburg PA
CBHW070000100426
42741CB00012B/3093